Will Grandberry III

THE AUTOPSY OF HOPE
Birthing Change Through Crisis

Literacy in Motion, Publishing

THE AUTOPSY OF HOPE
Birthing Change Through Crisis

Copyright by Will Grandberry III

All rights reserved. No portion of this book may be reproduced, scanned, stored in a retrieval system, transmitted in any form or by any means – electronically, mechanically, photocopy, recording or any other – except for brief quotations in printed reviews, without the written permission of the publisher.

The scanning, uploading, and distribution of this book without permission is a theft of the author's intellectual property. If you would like permission to use material from the book (other than for review purposes), please contact posttribune@hotmail.com. Thank you for your support of the author's rights.

Please do not participate in or encourage piracy of copyrighted materials in violation of the author's rights. Purchase only authorized editions.

Copy and Content Editing Anthony KaDarrell Thigpen of Literacy in Motion

www.LiteracyinMotion.ink
First Edition: October 2024

Library of Congress Cataloging-in-Publication Data
ISBN: 9 7 9 8 3 3 8 9 8 8 0 8 4

THE AUTOPSY OF HOPE

Christian Books/ Biographies/ General
Printed in the United States of America

ACKNOWLEDGEMENTS

I am deeply grateful to everyone who has supported me in creating this book.

To my family, whose unwavering love and encouragement have been my foundation, thank you. Also, to my parents for their wisdom and guidance, to my siblings for their committed and steadfast support, and to my generation, whose resilience and authenticity inspire me every day.

A heartfelt thank you to my editor, Anthony KaDarrell Thigpen, for your invaluable role in shaping this project. Your insightful feedback, dedication, and unwavering belief have been instrumental in bringing this book to life.

I thank my friends, colleagues, and every random person I met throughout this journey for their thoughtful feedback and encouragement. Your support has been invaluable.

I want to give special thanks to every Pastor, mentor, and inspirational figure whose work has guided me not only with this project but also with my overall purpose.

To my ancestors, whose legacy has paved the way and whose wisdom continues to guide me, and to future generations, for whom I hope this work will inspire hope and resilience—thank you.

And finally, to my readers, your interest and support mean the world to me.

With gratitude,
Will Grandberry III

A POETIC AUTOPSY OF HOPE

In a chamber dim and cold,
Where tales of sorrow are retold,
Lay hope, once radiant, now ceased,
For an autopsy to be released.

The examiner, with hands so sure,
Sought the cause, the obscure lure.
That drained hope's luminous glow,
Leaving it lifeless, lying low.

Inside, where dreams once danced free,
Were traces of melancholy.
The arteries, once pulsing with desire,
Now bore the scars of a quagmire.

Yet, as the autopsy neared its end,
A revelation did ascend:
Though hope seemed lifeless, it wasn't gone,
Its essence persisted, waiting for dawn.

For in the darkest, deepest night,
Hope's ember retains its light.
And with a spark, a gentle stroke,
It can rekindle, awake, provoke.

So, let not the autopsy deceive,
For hope, though dormant, will never leave.
In every heart, it finds a home,
A resilient force, forever to roam.

TABLE OF CONTENTS

Foreword
Dr. Jamal Bryant   pg. 6

Prologue
The Dissection   pg. 8

Introduction
The Dawn of Hope   pg. 12

Chapter 1
Dead on Arrival   pg. 20

Chapter 2
Benefit of the Doubt   pg. 32

Chapter 3
Fatal Distraction   pg. 45

Chapter 4
Bitter Disappointment   pg. 55

Chapter 5
Discouragement, Despair and Depression   pg. 71

Chapter 6
Discovery Channel   pg. 85

Chapter 7
Demonstration Hope   pg. 99

FOREWORD

Dr. Jamal Bryant

In a world where crises seem to multiply, where despair often outpaces hope, the need for a guide to navigate these turbulent times has never been more pressing. The Autopsy of Hope: Birthing Change in Crisis by Will Grandberry is not just a book; it is a beacon for those lost in the darkness of life's most challenging moments. This work offers a profound exploration of the human experience when confronted with the seemingly insurmountable forces of death, doubt, distraction, disappointment, and discouragement. Yet, it is also a testament to the resilience of the human spirit, the capacity for discovery, and the enduring power of hope.

In the pages that follow, Grandberry meticulously dissects the anatomy of crisis, revealing not just the causes of our suffering but also the hidden opportunities for growth and transformation. He takes us through the stages of despair, holding a mirror to our struggles while gently guiding us toward the realization that within every end lies the seed of a new beginning. Each chapter is a journey—through death and doubt, distraction and disappointment—culminating in discovering and demonstrating hope, not as a fleeting emotion, but as a powerful force for change.

This book does not shy away from the hard truths. It does not offer easy answers or quick fixes. Instead, it challenges the reader to engage deeply with their own pain, confront their doubts and fears head-on, and find within themselves the strength to birth change even in the most desperate circumstances. As you begin this journey through the anatomy of crisis, know you are not alone. The path may be difficult, but within these pages, you will find the practical tools to transform your despair into hope, your disappointment into determination, and your crisis into a catalyst for change.

Prologue
THE DISSECTION

"Wisdom is like a baobab tree; no one individual can embrace it."

– African Proverb

Long before I was born, hopelessness was systematic. Generations of people within our community were born into cycles. Survival was a priority. People had no blueprint, motivation, or resources to climb out of the pit of hopelessness. Individuals born in hopelessness settle for paycheck to paycheck, or any means of survival. They want to make ends meet, the ability to feed their families, and the security of knowing that their children will return home the way they left. Think about all the brilliant talent, dreams, inventions, and businesses all highjacked and hindered by the contaminated reality of systematic hopelessness.

It's a trap that leads to grandmothers raising grandchildren, the school to prison pipeline increasing amongst black boys, and education and economic disparities. Life was no crystal stairs. Yet, despite all the harsh social ills within society I still dare to believe. Locked in a deep deposit of unimaginable despair contains a small seed of hope.

Although, I must admit, the socioeconomic climate contributed to grave inequities and disadvantages. Yet, this climate never stopped the children from dreaming. Even though our school wasn't a charter school, space was created for children to communicate about their dreams. Students were often asked what they wanted to be when they grew up. Their aspirations motivated them to align their dreams and attitudes, believing that hope makes dreams come true.

Like so many others, perhaps you have outgrown the phase of dreaming and hoping. You possibly have accepted like my mother used to say, "It is what it is." Yet, if you would give me a chance, I would love to compel you to explore the possibility once more. Life is more than what you are currently experiencing. This is not all that there is - perhaps there is more. So, just as an autopsy seeks to uncover the cause of death, this book aims to identify key factors that contribute to the lethal corruption of natural hope. It exposes what affects our everyday lives and highlights solutions that allow readers to discover the redemption of hope in any circumstance.

Thus, we examine everyday scenarios that impact ordinary people. Our examination includes high rates of homicide, poverty, lack of education, broken family structures, and systemic racism. I believe historically we have reached a rare position in time to conduct a proper spiritual autopsy. *The Autopsy of Hope* will resurrect and reconcile what was lost due to dysfunction, distress, and premature death.

The goal of this book is to provoke the reader with the conviction necessary to become a change agent. You were born to make a difference. Read these words carefully: You are called to Crisis! My journey will reveal that through the challenges of my teenage upbringing in Chicago, even to the years of living in Washington, D.C., the power of my hope in God remains unaltered. Success is not attributed to any sole person but hope in God alone.

Despite all the overwhelming odds stacked against me, hope gave me a reason to rise above the chaos and take charge in pursuing the path created for me. So, this is not your typical church book. The intent is not just to detail the tragic decline of hope but also to discuss the real transformation of discovering real hope.

The first step in the process of any autopsy is the stage of dissection which involves a full investigation of the body. This meticulous examination process enables forensic specialists to calculate the data of the often-unknown causes of death. So, through this detailed examination of "Hope," we will take an audacious strive to gain a deeper understanding. This analytical approach will reveal the importance of hope and how essential it is to any person who exists on the earth.

This book will serve as your manual to reclaiming and recovering any ounce of hope that has deteriorated throughout your life. Each page offers a chance for courageous conversations within yourself about real-life circumstances. This is the confident truth that despite anything you are currently experiencing there is enough hope to make up for everything you lost. This book will serve as your reminder that your best days are ahead.

Introduction

DAWN OF HOPE

"Every morning is a new beginning."

– African Proverb

It was midnight, and a brisk breeze drifted through the open window on Saturday night, July 13, 2013. I sat glued to my television, anxious and nervous about the potential verdict that would soon be rendered concerning the conviction of George Zimmerman. Zimmerman, a zealous vigilante, was charged with murdering 17-year-old Black teenager Trayvon Martin.

Martin's death was more than a tragic loss of a young life; it had become a symbol of the racial injustices and deep-seated prejudices that still permeated society. As I watched, I couldn't help but feel the weight of history pressing down, knowing that the outcome of this trial would echo through communities and shape conversations about race and justice for years to come.

George Zimmerman's story was that of a self-appointed guardian of his neighborhood. On the night of the incident, without any witnesses, he claimed he suspected Trayvon Martin of being a delinquent, trespassing in the community where Zimmerman served as a security guard. But instead of calling the police, Zimmerman took the law into his own hands. His misguided sense of duty led to the murder of an innocent, unarmed teen.
The media dissected every moment of that fateful night, but the only person alive with a recollection of the actual events was Zimmerman. According to his account, he claimed to have protected his neighborhood from a perceived threat. But to many, Trayvon Martin was the only one without protection. He was just a

kid walking home from a convenience store, armed with a bag of Skittles and a can of iced tea.

The trial was a rollercoaster of emotions, with the prosecution painting Zimmerman as a reckless vigilante whose actions were fueled by racial profiling, while the defense portrayed him as a concerned citizen who acted in self-defense. As I watched the coverage, I felt a gnawing sense of injustice, a fear that Trayvon's death would be dismissed as just another statistic, his humanity reduced to a footnote in a tragic tale.

The nation held its breath as the jury deliberated. For those who had followed the case closely, the wait was excruciating. Each passing minute seemed to stretch into an eternity, the air thick with anticipation and dread. The verdict would be more than a legal decision. It would be a statement on whose lives were valued and whose voices were heard, especially in a system that often seemed indifferent to the cries of the marginalized.

In that room, illuminated by the soft glow of the television, I felt a profound connection to the countless others who were also watching, waiting, and hoping for justice. The breeze from the open window was a reminder of the world outside, a world that seemed both beautiful and cruel, full of potential yet plagued by injustice.

As the night wore on, I couldn't shake the image of Trayvon Martin, a young life full of promise, snuffed out too soon. His story, his name, had become a rallying cry for change: a symbol of the fight against racial inequality and the urgent need for reform. No matter what the verdict would be, Trayvon's legacy would endure, a testament to the resilience and strength of those who refuse to be silenced.

It wasn't just Trayvon's death that drained the hope out of people. I was 28 years old, living in the heart of Southeast D.C., where gun violence was the leading cause of death for Black teenage males. The constant trauma of hearing and witnessing crime provoked a strong sense of emotional fatigue and hopelessness. It is a level of hopelessness that comes from not knowing how to protect or help.

Then, I saw the photo of Trayvon Martin, a young Black teenager, slain in the grass on a rainy night. That image triggered an emotion I pray I never experience again. This case wasn't just about Trayvon; it was about my brother and the countless young men whose lives had been cut short from a life full of potential, purpose, and productivity.

As I watched the murder trial, skepticism filled my mind—a natural response for many Black people aware of this country's history. The trial was more than a legal battle; it reflected the systemic issues we face daily. The verdict would determine not only Zimmerman's fate but also send a message about whose lives were valued in our society. Trayvon's legacy became a rallying cry for justice and change, fueling our fight for a better future.

It felt like it should have been an obvious conviction: guilty on every count. Finally, the moment arrived. I sat up, moved to the edge of my couch, and folded my hands in a posture of prayer. The foreman stood and read the verdict. In just a few seconds, it felt like the entire city of D.C. fell silent. Then the words came: George Zimmerman was not guilty. In an instant, chaos erupted in the corridors of my apartment, and all I could do was cry.

I stood and walked around my small apartment, feeling hope seep out of my heart and spirit with every step. Trayvon was not just a teenager. I couldn't escape the pain, and I couldn't shake the grief. I was paralyzed by the pain of someone that I didn't know, but deep within I knew because in essence, Trayvon was me.

Being a byproduct of teenage parents, like so many kids raised in Chicago, the idea of hope was merely a word and a concept. For most of us in the community, life was about pure survival. We were born to work, wed, have a family, and die. Hope was an imaginative construct that distracted youth with an illusion of desire that seemed unattainable.

The climate was hostile toward the very idea or potential of hope. The only real goal for anyone born in the community was to leave, yearning for a place where one could have the audacity to hope and the courage to dream. Therefore, I find it crucial to define hope.

Hope is defined as a confident expectation and anticipation of a better outcome. While "wishing" and "hoping" express similar desires, they carry different shades of meaning. Wishing often implies a longing for something, no matter how unrealistic, like winning the lottery or losing weight without exercising. On the other hand, hope suggests a God-centered belief that what you desire is possible and will happen.

Many years ago, I found myself caught in a constant dichotomy. In my community and within the walls of my home, hope though often threatened, remained steadfast and ever-present. The struggle for me was embracing an aspect of hope that was never exemplified, which made it challenging to desire more out of life. I had a lot of information but always struggled with encountering a living inspiration.

So, as quickly as hope had brought me new opportunities, it teetered on the brink of uncertainty. Confusion and doubt flooded my mind and heart during this period, leaving me at a crossroads without a clear path forward. For me, like countless others, hope often hangs by a thread, leaving us desperate for support.

Hope is cemented in the certified promise that provokes simple truths like "You can make it", You can do it", and "Anything is possible". In these few chapters, you will see an interesting parallel to our everyday lives as believers of Jesus and the individuals in the Bible who left everything to follow Him.

The Gospel of Luke vividly depicts the viral aftermath of the chaos at Calvary, where an innocent man was brutally tortured and humiliated by the government without defense. To compound their grief, they discovered his body missing.

What do you do when all options seem exhausted? What happens when you feel abandoned by God? What does life mean without God, or in this case, without hope? In such moments, life offers only two choices: hope or despair. Jesus led a radical movement, with a promise that he would never leave them or forsake his people. He even urged people to abandon everything for a new cause. The shock of his death left them anxious, fearing they could be next. Without hope, people live life afraid of the future, with questions that so many people have found themselves pondering, "What will happen next in my life?"
So, out of everyone at the scene of the crime Luke presents a unique narrative to the account. Two individuals, Cleopas, and an unnamed companion, embark on a transformative mission from a place where hope seemed lost. They journeyed seven miles away to Emmaus. Imagine yourself stepping into the shoes of this

unnamed figure as we embark on an investigative journey. Together, we will conduct a detailed autopsy of *Hope*; to resurrect our conviction and reignite the passion needed to achieve our wildest dreams and fulfill our greatest visions.

Through the *Autopsy of Hope*, we will evaluate seven pivotal chapters that dissect the very essence of the power of hope. We will examine how death, doubt, distraction, disappointment, discouragement, discovery, and demonstration either contaminate or cultivate our lives.

I am eager for you to uncover the resilient, hope-filled version of yourself and to witness the incredible potential you are destined to fulfill.

Chapter 1

DEAD ON ARRIVAL

"When there is no enemy within, the enemies outside cannot hurt you."

– African Proverb

Luke 24:2-3

"They found the stone rolled away from the tomb, 3 but when they entered, they did not find the body of the Lord Jesus."

I remember the night like it was yesterday. I washed my clothes at the laundromat on Pennsylvania Ave. in Washington D.C. at about 10:30 pm. I was casually folding my last batch while watching CNN tally the votes on who would become the next President of the United States. The year was 2016 and the race was between Secretary of State Hilary Clinton and then Reality Star Donald Trump. It seemed that most Americans considered it a no-brainer that the well-experienced career politician Hilary Clinton would win the election in a landslide. The political climate was optimistic, especially after 8 years of leadership from America's first black president Barack Obama.

Hope infused the possibility of history being made in the election of the first woman President of the United States. Her opponent Mr. Trump represented everything many of us felt would be wrong for America. From the moment he descended on the escalator at Trump Towers to announce his candidacy his entire platform echoed controversy and division. He was reckless with his words, irresponsible with his influence, and a consistent agitator of fear within the cultural climate of America. The logical choice between the two was assumed to be abundantly clear. Yet, as I was preparing to leave and place my last shirts into the laundry bag an update appeared on the screen, Donald Trump was in the lead winning more states than predicted.

Suddenly, the very sight of reading the announcement shifted my entire mood from undeniable confidence to overwhelming nervousness. As an African American, I was in total shock and afraid. Then the unthinkable occurred Donald J. Trump was elected as the 45th President of the United States. For many, that was the day that Hope Died.

I remember the camera spanning the audience of Hillary supporters and witnessing their tears of disappointment and defeat. Social media was flooded with doom and pessimism. The results of this election served as a reality that hope can at times be subjective. Based upon the perception of one part of the country over the other, there was a general assumption that all of America shared the same hope of a progressive America. However, based upon the results that was certainly not the case. The election of Donald Trump destroyed any ounce of hope that was salvaged through the years of Obama and brought back to reality the truth that America was more racist and divided than ever.

I must admit that the results of the election came as no real surprise to African American voters. Historically, African Americans have had an interesting relationship with hope. Hope is often utilized in a variety of ways. On one hand, it is a mechanism used to manage the frustration of communities that have experienced decades of broken promises and disenfranchisement. African Americans have had to hold the fort down on maintaining civility in the streets and turning the other cheek. However, hope also provoked an unshakable confidence within a people to never settle for struggle when they were born to succeed. It was hope that motivated our enslaved ancestors who were incarcerated in the gravity of their condition to keep praying and fighting for freedom.

It was hope that provoked courage within young people during the civil rights movement to protest for voting rights and equality. It was this same hope that galvanized millions of Americans to twice elect a Black man into the highest office of our land. Yet, throughout all the years of historical evidence, the demonstrative power of this hope was assassinated the very moment Trump was declared the winner. There was no obituary but it was a sure moment in the lives of millions of Americans that hope died, and the idea of change was dramatically impossible.

What is life without hope? Like so many I was raised in the Black Church. I wasn't a part of any Black Church; I was a member of a Pentecostal church. The Church of God in Christ where we shouted, spoke in tongues, and did all the other peculiar things that usually go viral on social media. In our church, we would have testimony services where people would stand up with excitement expressing their hope in God but also would request prayer to see hope revealed in their personal lives. Living within the inner city of Chicago, faith was crucial to maintain sanity.

I was a unique kid who was extremely observant and inquisitive. I grew up attending Sunday School and learning about Jesus coming into the world to die for our sins. But one Sunday I had an interesting epiphany in real-time during an Easter service as the Pastor was closing out his sermon. The church was filled with so many people, the energy was magnetic, and the pastor yelled the infamous statement "he got up" referring to Jesus being resurrected from the dead. This statement provoked an electrifying response. People began running, jumping, and even crying at the phrase that we hear every year at Easter. People were full of enthusiasm and excitement, but I wondered was the expression a reaction to hope or if was it just hype. After all, what does "he got up" really mean?

Hope is defined as the confident expectation for a certain thing to happen. True hope can only be discovered in crisis. So, following that Sunday service, I began to investigate the psychosocial impact of the followers of Jesus the day he was publicly murdered by the hands of the government that were sworn to protect him. The first place I started the research for an accurate portrait of Christ was in the Gospel according to Luke. Luke's narrative serves as a forensic file and detailed investigative report on the full portrait of Jesus and the mission that he was born to fulfill. This investigation allows us to gather critical data sufficient for his followers to obtain the hope that he became on the earth so that we can impact the earth.

Jesus was seen as more than a miracle worker He was their hope. Everywhere he went there were viral moments of him healing the sick, feeding the hungry, and even performing miracles. His followers were chosen and told that the prerequisite to following him was to leave everything, and they did. This was their hope. For three years he taught, nurtured, and developed them into disciples. But then arrived the day that changed everything. This was the day their hope was held hostage on a cross. What do you do when the thing that you hoped for becomes the thing you hope it would never become?

I'm sure they had so many plans, expectations, and dreams of a nationalistic agenda of redemption for their people, but the moment occurred that crushed the movement. All their time and energy were seemingly thrown in the drain. Their anxiety increased because if the system could destroy the very person that they hoped was sent to overthrow it, certainly they could be next.

Everything happened in one night. The police captured an innocent Jesus in the middle of the night as he was praying. Who does that? They beat and tormented him all night. Jesus, was not only tortured but also publicly humiliated without cause or reason. The assault was so egregious that his body was disfigured beyond repair. Seemingly although this was public not one person interrupted the injustice and not one person mumbled a word. The only thing that those who followed him could do was watch the one they loved and in whom they placed their hope die. I can't even imagine the image, the rage, or even the shared trauma of a diminished dream being destroyed all in one day.

A 14-year-old boy from Chicago who, while visiting relatives in Mississippi in 1955, was brutally murdered by two white men after allegedly whistling at a white woman. His body was found disfigured, and his mother's decision to have an open-casket funeral exposed the horrors of racism to the world. Despite clear evidence, his killers were acquitted by an all-white jury but later admitted to the crime.

Emmett Till's body is a compassionate modern-day reminder of how mutilated the body of Christ was during crucifixion. In essence, it was not cute, or culturally appropriate. Imagine the scene of Jesus' crucifixion: the accusation of guilt, the relentless beatings, and the whips tearing into His back. Huge nails are driven into His hands and feet, and the crown of thorns presses deep into His scalp, with blood trickling down His face. Both were innocent, both were victims of unspeakable brutality, and both suffered to the point of being unrecognizable. The injustice in both cases is stark and heart-wrenching but their tragedy created a desperate hope that an unjust society could never break.

This is the case for many individuals in our world. Somewhere, their promise and dreams were crushed by the harsh reality of life.

Their hope didn't just die; it was destroyed, broken, beaten, and battered to the degree that what was once believed in can't even be recognized.

Can you imagine what is going through their minds? Can you imagine processing the realization that all your dreams and investments have crumbled without any proof of showing you had it in the first place? Can you factor in the grief of witnessing such a loss, the grudge toward the system that committed the offense, and the guilt of possibly being a spectator and not being more supportive in saving your only hope? This phase of life is called hopelessness.

These were the exact emotions experienced during my senior year of high school. I always stood out as different, smart, and unique, but in a community that emphasized conformity as the key to belonging, masculinity had no option but to conform. So, I became a class clown, thriving and struggling for attention and acceptance at the expense of my authenticity and identity.

My life took a dramatic turn one day when I encountered a teacher after school. I had been mimicking her, but when she unexpectedly threw me against a locker in frustration, it shattered my facade. The embarrassment was overwhelming—I ran out of the building, fearing my true self. I thought maybe my bad boy persona had been exposed and my cover was blown. I felt fearful that others would see that I wasn't as tough as I portrayed.

With a mediocre GPA of 2.4 and a dismal 12 on my ACT, the reality of being kicked out of school meant more than just losing an institution—it meant losing my future. My counselor expressed that the greatest option I had to be anything in life potentially would have to begin in a community college. With the reality of me being out of school, it felt like Hope died. At that moment, I saw myself becoming another statistic of the community, a failure before I even began. Yet, in the depths of despair, a flicker of real hope emerged.

From that day forward, I was determined to not just survive but to thrive. Suddenly, I remember receiving a letter in the mail from Howard University. No one in my family ever attended college I would be the first to attend and I was blown away just to receive any mail from a school with my name. It was weird because I never applied to any school because I was afraid of rejection. However, one day my mother opened the mail and the words read Congratulations you have been accepted. The kid who was once facing expulsion was now reading in bold that I was Accepted. I had been rejected most of my life but to be Accepted was a feeling that to this day I will never forget. It was there that I realized that the moment my hope died was the day my life began.

Death is often something that we don't like to discuss particularly at certain phases of our lives. Yet, it is the only inevitable construct of assurance in life; anything that is born will die. Social media has created a virtual dungeon for entitlement and unrealistic expectations. Based on your engagement of the platform it can influence you in ways that we often don't realize. So, sometimes we develop desires and goals for things that are not aligned with our "true identity." We want "things" because of a variety of reasons that will boost our ego.

In the autopsy of hope, we confront the uncomfortable reality that some forms of hope were never truly alive—they were manufactured illusions shaped by the expectations and pressures of a world that prizes image over substance. Social media, with its endless scroll of curated perfection, has exacerbated this, creating a space where we chase desires that may not even belong to us. We long for validation, success, and material symbols of status, mistaking these for hope when, in truth, they are nothing but distractions. The death of this kind of hope is necessary. It must be laid to rest so that we can strip away the layers of ego and entitlement that cloud our vision, forcing us to confront what is truly worth hoping for. The death of these superficial hopes clears the path for something real, rooted not in what we want to be seen as but in who we genuinely are.

Hope placed in anything other than God isn't really hope at all. Sometimes, God's love for you means letting certain hopes or dreams fade away so that you can discover the faithful Hope that lasts forever. This kind of Hope shifts your perspective and helps you realign your focus. Take in these words: "Nothing you've ever lost is wasted." While we can't deny that death is painful, a deeper look at our lives reveals that something had to end for us to become who we are today.

Chapter 2

BENEFIT OF THE DOUBT

"When you show the best of yourself, even when others do not believe in you, you are creating a path for the future."

– African Proverb

Luke 24:12

"Peter, however, got up and ran to the tomb. Bending over, he saw the strips of linen lying by themselves, and he went away, wondering to himself what had happened."

Doubt, like a silent shadow, creeps into our minds, chipping away at our hopes and dreams. It whispers uncertainties, questions our worth, and challenges our beliefs. In a technologically advanced era such with Artificial Intelligence (AI), information has shaped the social construct of generations, providing limitless information. Unlike previous generations, no more television shows preserve children's innocence like "Mr. Rogers." This present generation has been robbed of the beauty of mystery and the unique power of imagination. Although inconceivable to some, Generation Z and beyond have never known life without the Internet. Through the exposure of platforms like social media, the plight of systemic injustice and historical challenges loom, and the notion of doubt can be particularly pervasive and paralyzing.

The forensic scene was emotionally intense after reports came back from the women who arrived at the grave site of Jesus. Upon arrival, they realized the harsh conclusion that the body they were preparing to preserve was missing. Yes, you read that right. They showed up with one agenda but realized that God had another. What do you do when faith in one thing doesn't match the facts? There is nothing worse than being in your house and losing your keys. I'm a bit emotional, so when an ounce of doubt kicks in, I naturally react and rip my entire house into shreds. I'm sure this was Peter's emotional response when he heard the news that the Body of Jesus was missing. Who steals a body? Where is the funeral director? For Peter, this was not a resurrection. This was a raw reality. Hope is Gone.

Peter rushed to the grave site to witness for himself, and the first thing he noticed was the linen that covered Jesus in the grave. There was evidence with no explanation - this moment changed everything. The autopsy revealed that one of the primary killers of hope is doubt. Doubt undermines the confidence and belief necessary for hope to thrive. Doubt diminishes the motivation to strive for anything more significant than average. Can you imagine the mental anguish and perplexity Peter experienced? Upon arrival, he realized that everything he'd hoped for over the past three years was brutally destroyed in just three days. To make matters worse, Jesus was missing.

Etched in the process of grief is the strong influence of doubt. Sometimes, individuals find it challenging to come to terms with the fact that a loved one has died. Or delusion may cause it to be difficult to even accept the negative outcome of something desperately expected. However, within every crisis, there is a choice between coping in denial or confronting the doubt. The evidence of linen in the tomb eliminated the expectation of the embedded goal that their hope would never be fulfilled in Jesus. Any idea of assuming a return from the dead was dismissed because there was no physical body present. I can't even imagine the psychological tension of reconciling what he saw with what he previously believed. Peter's experience perfectly mirrors our battles with doubt, especially in a society where truth often feels obscured by injustice and inequality.

The Disease of Doubt

Doubt begins with a specific thought. These thoughts are seeds in the mind, planted by personal experiences, societal influences, and systemic dysfunctions. Our imagination is a powerful tool for creativity and resilience. It can also be co-opted with doubt, making us question even our most deeply held beliefs. It was the spring semester in my first-year English literature class at Howard University when I first experienced real doubt. I was already nervous about being around so many intelligent college kids from around the country. I attended a decent High School, it was precisely that, descent. One day, I decided to speak up, offering my perspective on our conversation. I remember the awkward silence that hovered over the room as I finished. I remember this random girl turning back to me in the most condescending view and responding, "What is he trying to say, yawl?" the entire class laughed.

Time could not move slower at the level of embarrassment at this moment. I remember having a mental war on deciding whether I should ever speak again in public. It was clear that doubt has the unique propensity to provoke conflict within your courage. Had I surrendered to doubt, I would have forfeited destiny.

Such is the case in the heart of Chicago, as with inner cities across America, where the echoes of gunshots and sirens are a daily soundtrack to urban life, the lethal power of doubt is integrated as an essential commodity of culture. For many, the city's vibrant culture is overshadowed by systemic oppression, economic disparities, failing schools, and historical injustices. This environment of dysfunction fosters a profound lack of trust in our surroundings—whether it's due to broken promises, systemic oppression, or the absence of evidence that things will ever change. Living in such conditions is like an urban version of Hunger Games where the easiest way to stay alive is simple... DON'T TRUST ANYONE.

Persistent doubt leads to a pessimistic mindset, fostering negative thinking and toxic behavior. For those who are disadvantaged, this pervasive doubt can erode self-worth and stifle ambition. It's easy to internalize these shortcomings and doubt your potential. This psychological burden of doubt becomes a barrier, not just to personal success but to the collective hope and progress within the community.

The Dysfunction of Doubt

Doubt is not just a personal struggle—it's generational and societal. Distrust has been passed down through generations, rooted in historical injustices and ongoing systemic failures. This deep-seated skepticism thrives when those meant to protect and guide us become sources of suspicion. I grew up in a period where we were warned against "stranger danger," cautioning against trusting people we didn't know. This distrust increased anxiety and fear within the overall outlook of life, which was rooted more in fear than the future.

For some people in America, this hope never existed. This reality is revealed through decades of blatant systemic failures in education, healthcare, housing, and employment that are rampant in communities of color. In addition, these schools are underfunded, healthcare access is limited, housing conditions are poor, and job opportunities are scarce. These pervasive failures make upward mobility a daunting challenge, further fostering doubt and distrust. Thus, the climate of distrust reduces the idea of motivation. In these circumstances, there is no faith in future possibilities because the very concept of hope is just a way to cope.

Thus, what do we expect from a community that survives without expectations? Politicians and leaders often make grand promises for change that remain unfulfilled. When pledges for better living conditions, safety, and opportunities repeatedly fall through, the community's trust in these figures erodes. People naturally begin to doubt the sincerity and capability of those in power, reinforcing a cycle of skepticism.

The deaths of prominent individuals at the hands of police have stirred riots and increased this deep-seated distrust and hopelessness. George Floyd's death in May 2020, after a Minneapolis police officer knelt on his neck for over nine minutes, sparked worldwide protests and riots, highlighting the persistent issue of police brutality against Black Americans. Similarly, Breonna Taylor's fatal shooting by police in Louisville during a botched raid in March 2020 led to widespread protests and demands for accountability. There is a list of countless others who had to accept that hope is not here.

The repeated instances of police violence without accountability continue to fuel doubt and hopelessness within urban communities. Maintaining hope or keeping a positive outlook on life becomes a daily struggle in such environments. Merely existing is difficult enough as a minority in America. It's another train of thought when that individual expects something different from what doubt pre-determined.

Curing the Contamination
Doubt doesn't just challenge our trust in external entities; it also seeps into our most personal relationships. It contaminates our dependence on God, our families, and life itself. Like Peter, there are many within generations of society who, I'm sure, possessed in their hand the evidence of something they once believed in but had to accept that it no longer exists.

Just trace the history of the Jewish people up to this point in time. They were once chosen people with a track record of conquering -

all they did was win. They were the owners of land and riches and the governing authority of that region. However, through the invasions of Babylon, Israel experienced a significant scattering and separation. Fortunate individuals returned to their homeland but had to submit to another authority, Rome. This is important because generations of individuals, past and present, still await this exact hope. This is how intense it was for those following Jesus during that time. They believed he was God and that he would overthrow the government so that they may overcome the grief of being in the minority.

So, Peter's discovery at the cemetery reflects the real climate of inner cities around America. A distrust in one thing can lead to a distrust in everything. Being born into a family of teenage parents had its share of advantages and disadvantages. The outstanding advantage was growing up with young parents full of life and energy. The disadvantage was that I inherited their doubts. For example, my parents loved people, but they didn't have a lot of friends. Their trust in people was short, and they had low expectations of anyone aside from one another. The consequence of such a persistent perspective of pessimism was its impact on my relationships. Doubt kept my heart closed and forced me to always live on the defense. Doubt paralyzed my ability to be vulnerable or believe anyone truly liked or loved me.

Doubt is also infectious. The correct number of questions will cause anyone to question what they once believed. Peter, was caught on three separate occasions and questioned of his allegiance with Jesus and with each inquiry he denied it because he doubted the outcome would be favorable. Thus, this is the case in this generation. Despite all the positive information available and the access to resources to enhance their lives, there is a group who refuse to release the remains of what no longer exists.

We begin to wonder if our dreams are valid or if we should even pursue them. I remember the moment I got into Howard University. The energy and emotions were unmatched, considering that I never applied to get in. So, I went through the acceptance package but noticed that the information needed to be included regarding housing was not included. The missing information caused me to contact the University. I contacted the school to gain clarity. I was told that I was accepted but Unclassified. Huh? What does that even mean? In other words, I could come to school but couldn't participate or live on campus. Wait, I'm not even from D.C.; I knew no one in the area. I remember the anxiety formed like wildfire. I begin to panic and rethink my entire life. Doubt can debilitate you. It has a way of creating fear that can stop you from pursuing purpose prematurely because of false perceptions.

So, I took my chances and continued to call them, but to my surprise, the counselor changed his mind and changed my status.

My testimony is that I entered campus with kids who were wealthier, wiser, and more advanced, but I graduated with two bachelor's degrees in four years. I eventually had an epiphany that the greatest way to defeat doubt is to doubt your doubts. What if everything you need to change your life is behind the simple "what if"? Not, what if you Fail but what if you succeed? For every moment spent dwelling in doubt, spend the same time dreaming of your destiny.

Overcoming Self-Doubt

Self-doubt is the most debilitating form of doubt. It hampers our progress, stifles our creativity, and prevents us from achieving our full potential. Overcoming self-doubt requires us to challenge our negative beliefs, embrace our strengths, and build a supportive network that reinforces our self-worth. While doubt is the enemy of hope, it also has the potential to be a catalyst for growth and more profound understanding when mixed with optimism and determination. By learning to navigate the murky waters of doubt, we can emerge stronger, with a renewed sense of hope. Instead of doubting yourself, give yourself the benefit of the doubt and never settle until you discover the evidence.

I remember a field trip with my father that taught me a valuable lesson about doubt. He had promised to join me, but he was nowhere in sight as the bus was about to leave. My emotions surged—embarrassment, confusion and a growing sense of doubt in his reliability. However, when we reached our destination, he was there waiting for us, having arrived before we did. This experience made me realize that not all doubts are based on truth; some are illusions created by our insecurities and past disappointments.

Doubt is powerful. Yet, even in its shadow, doubt can lead to positive outcomes. It pushes us to seek more proof, to dive deeper, and to explore further. This relentless pursuit of certainty can ultimately lead us to stronger, more resilient hope, not just the hope we formed in our imagination.

So, before you panic, relax. Doubt is a natural human response to life uncertainties. Doubt just simply means you don't have all the details. I don't care who you are; we all experience moments of doubt. The challenge is what to do with those doubts, which will determine the benefits. Peter doubted, which provoked him to seek Jesus himself.

In examining the broader themes of doubt and hope in this book, "benefit of the doubt" is about pushing forward to exhaust your options without giving up, no matter the situation. It's about maintaining a balanced perspective, acknowledging uncertainties, and seeking truth with an open mind. Doubt can be both a hindrance and a motivator. I doubt that doubt has enough power to cause you to give up. Maybe your present doubts are not to confuse or concern you. Maybe these doubts are divinely orchestrated to discover a greater hope within you - a genuine hope that will never die and never be destroyed. Here's some advice: it's your responsibility to keep searching relentlessly until you uncover evidence proving that hope is still very much alive. Even when it feels elusive or distant, don't stop looking for the signs, the moments, and the experiences that confirm hope's presence. It may take time and effort but discovering hope's persistence will be worth the journey.

Chapter 3
FATAL DISTRACTION

"A bird will always use another bird's feathers to build its nest."

– African Proverb

Luke 24:15

"As they talked and discussed these things with each other, Jesus himself came up and walked along with them; 16 but they were kept from recognizing him."

Like doubt, distractions can make your journey even more difficult. When doubt enters your mind, then distraction spreads through your heart. Distraction is a sneaky enemy. It quietly shifts our attention from our goals, messes up our progress, and breaks our focus. Staying focused on our hopes and dreams is challenging in our noisy world. My favorite sport to watch is basketball, but only during the playoffs or finals. What I often find interesting is that when a player is fouled and prepares for a free throw, the stadium is never quiet. It's typically the loudest in that moment. The opposing team aims to distract the player from focusing on the goal. In other words, focus will never be an absence of noise; it is one's ability to maintain attention despite the noise. Distractions contribute to many destiny-altering infractions, and we can all empathize with the struggles that come from distractions.

The emotions were high, and the frustration amongst his disciples was unmanageable. The tragedy of the moment was so intense that many followers of Jesus walked away to escape the scene. The entire event was so traumatic that the people left the same day. They wanted no part of what had occurred, possibly because the same thing that happened to Jesus could happen to them. Their reaction wasn't weird; it was real. They could not comprehend or make sense of anything that transpired that day. So, the longer they entertained doubt, the more desperate and distracted they became, and the weight of their situation became overwhelmingly intense.

A variety of reasons triggers distractions, the most particularly being a lack of focus due to anxiety and stress. Our neighborhood had some peculiar dynamics growing up. We lived on a block where we had several burglaries. However, the strange thing about the community is that we typically knew who the offender was. So, the knowledge of that reality always caused me to enter the house with hesitation because of the distrust of security in the area. One day, my mother asked me to go in the house to grab her purse, and man, it was at night, and my internal alert system was on high. I had a mission to get in and out as quickly as possible. So, I went into the house and ran upstairs and as soon as I reached the top, I saw something that looked like a person. I am unapologetically black, and I did what any of my cousins would do. I RAN! I went downstairs to get my mother to let her know that somebody was in our house. She came with me, and to our surprise, when she turned on the lights, a suit jacket on a vacuum was standing there. WOW!

Distractions often lead us to focus on what's in front of us rather than what truly matters - this was the case for the followers of Jesus. They left because they couldn't accept the truth that the person, they had placed all their hope in was no longer with them due to the crucifixion. It's a sobering reminder of how our emotional responses to life's changes can lead us astray. Do we stay committed to our original goals, or do we give in to the belief that things will never improve? Both choices come with a cost that can shape our entire lives.

Where Do Distractions Come From?

In today's fast-paced world, distractions are an unavoidable part of life. It's important to note that not all distractions are negative. Sometimes, positive things can divert us from our top priorities. Distractions can stem from anxiety and stress, lack of interest, and mental fatigue. One of the most significant distractions in our modern world is social media. The societal addiction to cell phones has become a norm in schools and local homes, even at the dinner table. Even children are born and raised to have their tablets to aid in their distractions. We must understand that what captures their attention at a young age will continue to do so as they grow into adults. Distractions become conditioned responses to individuals who doubt the reality of destiny. The most challenging aspect of distractions is that they don't always appear to be distractions.

An unidentified distraction was the case for the individuals who left Jerusalem. The only subject of conversation was the events that had just occurred. The more you discuss the dynamics of doubts, the more distracted you become by them. Jesus' death was the talk of the town; they were consumed by this crisis and had no clarity of what to do next. The only thing that they can do is walk the opposite way of where they were supposed to be. They were distracted by the doubts that he died, and no one could determine why this had to happen.

Distractions are dangerous and can force you to lose things you may not recover. I wasn't the smartest or most athletic in high school. I ran track, and the dangers of distractions became clearer. One day, as I was running the 400-meter dash, I was on it with a clear focus on the finish line, and right when I thought I was about to finish, the first distraction appeared. I was doing well and making great strides, but then a runner who looked like an adult in the wrong league appeared. I became so fixated with his presence next to me that I lost sight of the prize and lost the race. One distraction can cost your entire destiny.

Focus matters more than speed. Distractions are all around us, and what we focus on will gain the most power - it's a choice. Until we understand that anyone or anything with our focus also has our future, we'll continue to be at the mercy of distractions. These men were walking away from where they believed their hope would be fulfilled because the person, they had hoped for proved to be just a man. The question isn't about where they left. The real question is who they left behind. It's astonishing how much responsibility we neglect because of distractions. The value of our choices, especially regarding focus, cannot be overstated.

Delays, Detours, and Deviations

Delays sometimes trigger distractions. Delays are a daily expectation in Washington, DC, particularly on the BW Parkway. I don't care what time you get on the expressway; it's a definite guarantee you will get stuck in traffic and delayed arriving at your next appointment. Sometimes, God uses delays as detours to get to your destination. However, we must remain focused and avoid becoming so consumed by the frustrations of being delayed that we never miss the destination.

I'm not too fond of delays; they are frustrating. Like many people in my generation, we associate the measure of success and goals we should have achieved with age. New-aged cultural standards dictate that by the time we reach a certain age, we should be successful. However, as you know, if you have lived more than a year on earth, life has a way of spinning precise curb balls and redirecting our paths when it wants to do whatever it wants. I was 27 years old, a recent graduate of Howard Divinity School, when I was accepted a student career employment position in the state department. I was so excited that the kid with three earned degrees finally arrived on the federal side with great benefits. They began assigning all the roles to my peers and waited until the end to provide my profile position.

I watched the reaction of all my fellow students get excited about going to the top floors. Then my folder came, and it said EX, meaning executive suite. I automatically thought I had arrived, as in achieved success, until my floor was four instead of seven like my peers. Surprisingly, I ended up sorting mail in the mail room. Wait, remember, I thought I had arrived. I had high "hopes" that I would come in as a boss. Yet, I ended up being the mailman for at least a year in the basement of the statement department. Let me be clear there is nothing wrong with being a mailman, it was just far away from upper management. I became so disgusted and distracted by the unbelief of being in this position that I never qualified my journey as the necessary delay that destined me for the right opportunity.

One day, I shifted my focus from being distracted to being determined to do a great job. Instead of focusing on where I was, I began working on who I wanted to become. I saw a profile highlighting the Office of International Religious Freedom. I met the Ambassador on my lunch break, and somehow, I ended up on the 7th floor with the rest of my peers because of the delayed detour. Sometimes, we become so distracted by our delays that, like the disciples, we quit without realizing that this is the exact route required to get to an unimaginable place. Read this slowly, you are right where you are supposed to Be, Right Now!
Jerusalem is the place of their faith, the place of their birth, and the place of their entire hope. The followers were so distracted by what they saw and heard that they didn't even remember what they had learned. Unbeknownst to them, Jesus was walking with them the

entire time, but the text highlights God didn't allow them to recognize him. God doesn't just reveal he also restricts. Sometimes he restricts things that you may want to keep you focus on what you really need. Wait, what type of sci-fi saga is this? You read it correctly: the person they were mourning was moving with them even as they were leaving the place of what they considered to be defeat.

Distraction can take you down rabbit holes that you never intended to visit. You don't realize it until you are stuck in a deviated with defeat. Detours are often routes used because of destination delays. When distractions take hold, they can lead us to a series of setbacks that pull us away from our intended paths. These setbacks often manifest as deviations and defeat. We all have a planned route that we desire to pursue. Sometimes, the path becomes apparent only once a crisis occurs. It's in these difficult situations that we gain revelation of the course. However, it is important to use discernment and stay focused.

Deviations happen when our focus shifts from primary objectives to secondary or unrelated concerns. This shift in focus can pull us away from our core objectives, leading us to deviate from the path we initially set for ourselves. When you lose sight of the plan, instead of producing, you procrastinate. How far could you have been without distractions? How many goals could have been met if not for distractions? Defeat is the ultimate consequence of being consistently sidetracked by distractions. When detours and deviations accumulate, they can erode our motivation and confidence. The constant barrage of media sensationalism and political discord can create a sense of hopelessness, making it challenging to stay positive and driven. The emotional and mental toll of these distractions can lead to feelings of defeat, where we feel overwhelmed and unable to reach our goals. Distracted by the wrong attraction can be fatal, ask Samson.

Distractions are like hidden toxins within the body of life, insidiously creeping in and spreading through the bloodstream of our thoughts. Just as an autopsy reveals the underlying causes of death, a deep examination of our disappointments often uncovers distractions as the silent killers of our dreams. These distractions, whether digital temptations or societal pressures, divert our focus, corroding the vital organs of ambition and perseverance. Over time, they lead to the slow decay of purpose, leaving behind the hollow shell of unfulfilled potential. Only through dissecting these distractions can we identify their corrosive impact and reclaim control over the direction of our lives. Don't lose focus because the lack of focus will cause you to lose yourself!

Chapter 4
BITTER DISAPPOINTMENT

"When the roots of a tree begin to decay, it spreads death to the branches."

- African Proverb

Luke 24:21

"But we were hoping that it was He who was going to redeem Israel. Indeed, besides all this, today is the third day since these things happened."

Disappointment is the incision that reveals the wounds beneath the surface. It often begins with distraction—a subtle shift of focus that cuts away at our dreams. When we lose sight of our purpose, life's disappointments come into sharp focus, like the cold steel of a scalpel. Like most people, I've had to endure a series of disappointments.

After taking a road trip with some of my college friends, I remember the blissful emotion of returning from Chicago to Washington D. C. It was summertime and the fact that we were all from the same hometown made the trip incredibly epic. My friend pulled up to my apartment and though the neighborhood wasn't ideal nothing could shake the sense of pride that I had being that it was my first apartment. I called it home. I encouraged my friends to park so that I can provide them with a quick tour of my one-bedroom unit to emphasize my newly obtained independence. But to my shocking surprise when I walked up the stairs, I noticed something weird and strange, the door was cracked. Suddenly, a subtle nervous feeling hit the center of my gut instinctively signaling that something was wrong.

I was hesitant but wanted to maintain my composure based on the company that was with me. With each step, I was secretly hoping that either my eyes were deceived, or that through negligence I simply forgot to lock the door by mistake. Yet, the moment I faced the door I realized that my place had been burglarized and everything was gone. I sat there in this small unit surrounded by nothing in utter awe. Someone broke into the apartment and stole every item from the closet, and they even managed to take the hotdogs from the refrigerator. I'm not making this up this is a true story.

So, in this small empty apartment, I stood supported by friends while plagued with a variety of emotions. I was numb, I didn't know the proper response. I was embarrassed, angry, and traumatized all at the same time. Now, I was not new to criminality including break-ins but nothing prepares a person for things like this to happen to them. I was in a city 11 hours away from home, and so security and safety were extremely important.

So, I called the police, and they filed a report. They finished their investigation and to my surprise, they dared to state that I was safe to stay in the apartment for the night. Are you kidding me? There was no way I was going to trust anything and anybody to stay in a place that was just raided by strangers. Naturally, my mind went into fight or flight mode. Will the burglar return when I sleep? Was someone watching me when I left to go on the road trip? The very notion of pre-existing danger provoked me to create natural distance.

This was the reality of the two men who experienced the traumatic site of Jesus dying on the cross. After realizing that their hopes and life expectations had been destroyed their emotions naturally spiraled. The Bible never gives us an actual detailed reaction or case study toward the response of the disciples besides Peter, Thomas, and Judas. Yet, emotionally they were broken and utterly disappointed. Their response to disappointment was distance.

As we continue this *Autopsy of Hope*, you'll discover how each disappointment carves its way into the human spirit. Disappointment settles into the soul like a spreading infection. This is the pattern: doubt begins in the mind, distractions enter the heart, and disappointment embeds itself in the soul. Disappointment is simply an emotion of displeasure that is caused by the non-fulfillment in ones hope or expectation.

The followers were told by associates that the grave was empty and what they came to see was not what they expected. The degree of disappointment that was experienced at hearing about the murder and now missing case of Jesus was unmatched. So, instead of hiding and surviving in danger they went 7 miles away to established distance that wouldn't remind them of their disappointments.

Disappointment is a form of misplaced hope—a misalignment between what we desire and what we experience. While disappointment is an inevitable part of life, how we choose to process and address it shapes our journey forward. Disappointment often grows from distractions, leading us to place our faith in people or things that never made promises. How many of us remain loyal to what can never fulfill us? I've realized that sometimes God allows things to die to help us realize what truly lives.

This was the case for Isaiah who was only a scribe within the time of King Uzziah, but it was only when King Uzziah died that he was able to see the Lord. I believe that God allows things to happen to make other things happen. What are some things and some people that you can recall God is causing to be stopped in order that you may start believing again? God uses disappointment not to deny you but to develop you with the discipline of depending on him.

Coping with Life's Cuts
Throughout my personal life and professional career, I've understood that direction is essential for achievement. I believe that living within a set of goals and values are critical to healthy living. Yet, throughout my life I've faced significant disappointments along the way. I know I'm not alone in having moments where I feel that I should be further than where I am and certainly should be doing more than what I am doing.

Sometimes it feels as if God is hating on our goals. For instance, by age 30, I envisioned myself married with children living in a big house with a dog and picket fence. I want like everyone else the American Dream. Yet, like so many we are left only with our dreams which inevitably become nightmares. Distance often shift perception. Thus, the further you are away from the danger the more delusion settles to adapt to being disappointed. Disappointment that is unconfronted can become a personality.

Disappointment is the most heard soundtrack in the lives of Millennials. Our entire lifespan we have sat in the pool of cultural disappointment. Living through events like the beaten of Rodney King, the killing of Latasha Harlin, the missing ballots of Al Gore, the terrorist attack of September 11th, the Columbine shooting, levees broke in New Orleans through Hurricane Katrina, and the invasion of Iraq for "weapons of mass destruction, to name a few. For almost 40 years a generation has been nurtured in the apathetic sorrow of disappointment.

Let the record reflect, that national events contributed greater stress and systematic dysfunction to the already existing disenfranchised community. Therefore, disappointment no longer requires an event, but it has become a normalized emotion within an environment of failed expectations. Not having enough money to feed a family is disappointing. Having more police than people within a community but not knowing the name of the suspect that murdered is disappointing. Having more gas stations than grocery stores is disappointing. No longer being able to play outside for fear of young kids shooting is disappointing. And like most if they don't create distance from the environment, they become distant within their emotion and become numb.

My struggle to confront these disappointments directly has at times, hindered my growth. The trauma of mistrust has deeply affected me, making vulnerability an ongoing battle. Unfortunately, individuals that exist within the present often pay the price of the disappointment from people of my past. Even minor disappointments have often left me questioning the underlying reasons, preventing me from fully processing and moving past them. Like many people, I experienced challenges trying to understand the intentions of not only the "who but most importantly the "why."

Before we move forward and dissect the nature of discouragement in the next chapter, it's crucial to perform a thorough autopsy on the origins of disappointment. This examination reveals that disappointment is not a singular affliction but a complex condition that grows from three distinct roots: the disappointments life hands us, the wounds inflicted by others, and the deep scars we carve into ourselves. Each of these roots intertwines, creating a web that, if left unchecked, can suffocate our hope, and stifle our growth.

There were moments in my life when disappointment left me feeling as if my legs had been broken—paralyzed, trapped within myself, and utterly lost. The weight of disappointment can be so heavy that it drains the very life out of you. This sensation mirrors the experiences of Dr. King during the civil rights movement, where delayed hope felt like an unbearable burden.

Dr. Martin Luther King, Jr.'s life and death illustrate the impact of deferred hope in modern times. King faced obstacles and setbacks during the civil rights movement, from violent attacks to systemic injustices. Clearly, Disappointment became his middle name. Yet, despite these challenges, he maintained hope for racial equality and justice, symbolizing perseverance amid ongoing disappointment. The gap between desired change and reality can lead to frustration and despair. As King said, "Disappointment is a part of life, but confronting it with determination can turn setbacks into progress."

Disappointments Life Hands Us
One of my movies is Forest Gump, and in challenging times, He would reference quotes stated by his mother, and one of them was the infamous, "Life is like a box of chocolates. You never know what you are going to get." In other words, life is full of disappointment. What disappoints us most is the picture in our head of how we envision it is supposed to be. Yet, we quickly realize that life often happens beyond our control.

Throughout this book, I frequently revisit my childhood and upbringing because many of the wounds we carry as adults are rooted in the early years of our lives. To truly understand the twists and turns of deferred hope, I need to open windows into my past, allowing us to examine where these deep cuts began. Three sets of grandmothers surrounded me, and in their eyes, I was the golden child—the only boy and, for a time, the only grandchild. By age five, I was directing the choir, showered with praise, and held in high regard. But that attention slowly shaped me into a self-consumed and conceited perfectionist, seeping into every part of my life. Even down to the anxiety I felt playing video games, I could never accept a loss; I failed to process the normalcy of disappointment at an early age.

When I wasn't accepted into certain magnet schools, or even as recently as me being denied graduate school it was more than a disappointment—it felt like a personal failure. Depending on how you process disappointment it can make you into either an optimist or pessimist. For me it is the latter. There are moments that I'm afraid of great days because the trauma from previous disappointments reminds me not to get my hopes up, as in life can only become so good. Expecting disappointment usually becomes a toxic means of existence. So, I learned to anticipate disappointment to deal with the distrust it created even amongst those closest to me.

Let Downs from Others

Unexpected disappointments along the way have been a constant reminder of my destiny. Often, these disappointments arise from misplaced expectations—believing that others should be like us or that life should unfold in a certain way. There is a tendency to assume that society was all raised by the same mother and share the same goals. However, life will quickly remind you that is not the case. We set ourselves up for heartbreak when our expectations don't align with reality. I never struggled with having friends as a person, it was more of the kind of friends that I attracted that was the real concern.

I must admit my Parents did an amazing job of raising their children to have empathy and love all people. The constant disappointment robbed me of the courage to speak out or fight back when it came to defending myself. I would usually consider even the feelings of my offender and internalize the disappointment rather than confront it and move on. Rather than creating healthy boundaries I brought individuals completely into my world without any qualifiers or a critical assessment conducted. Thus, individuals would do whatever I allowed. Until I realized the pattern. There was a Wound in me that was unchecked that allowed me to always feel the need to set myself on fire while I kept others warm. I realized that the reason I was so accessible was that I wanted to be accepted. Don't allow the cycle of Disappointments cause you to lose your Dignity.

Thus, it's through the revelation of the root of the disappointment that I was able to identify the power I gave to anyone in my life. I had a friend who, in the end, proved to be untrustworthy. Despite past disappointments, a part of me still longed for connection, a circle of friends I could rely on.

I invited this friend on an overseas trip, making sure to call daily, confirming plans, and ensuring everything was set. But he canceled the day we were scheduled to fly, leaving me alone to travel to another country. I remember sitting on the beach and examining my entire life of people that were in my circle. I made everyone a suspect because of one situation and because I was disappointed by one friend. That single act of betrayal was like a scalpel, cutting into my sense of trust and shaping how I viewed others. It revealed how disappointment can be contagious, spreading its infection to our perceptions and interactions with others.

It's easy to let the pain pile up when we experience back-to-back disappointments, especially at the hands of those we trust. This accumulation of wounds can make us blame the individuals involved and God, questioning why these hurts continue.

In this *Autopsy of Hope*, it's essential to recognize that the wounds inflicted by others often leave deep scars. These emotional cuts can lead to a cycle of mistrust, where we begin to see everyone through the lens of our past pain. We become hyper-vigilant, always on guard, expecting others to let us down. Although it may appear comfortable the truth is without hope you are not healthy. This defense mechanism is natural but can also isolate us, preventing the connections we long for. To heal, we must first acknowledge the impact others have had on our lives, understanding that while their actions may have wounded us, we don't have to carry the infection of disappointment forever.

Deep Scars We Carve into Ourselves

I had an image of myself created by others, and I desperately needed to live up to it. At 16, I was preaching, and by 23, I was ordained, yet I was living a double life, torn between who I was and who I felt I needed to be. This conflict brought about a deep sense of disappointment within me, much like the disciples who, after Jesus' death, felt as if hope had died with him. They became distracted by their disappointment, unable to see that Jesus was still with them, listening.

While most disappointments are manageable in that it is caused by others, my greatest battle with disappointment has been with the scars I've carved into myself. There is no feeling in the world worse than the feeling of regret. It's the knowledge of making a vow or setting a goal and breaking it. It's essential to remain true to your authentic self; disappointment hits harder and hurts worse than the pain that comes from people. Statements like, "I should have said No," "I could've just stayed on course," and "I would've had more had I not brought those shoes."

Disappointment is painful. With most pain individuals find ways to cope rather than confront. Personally, for me, the way I dealt with disappointment was particularly in the realm of perversion and pornography. I started believing my past sins had sealed my fate. I thought what nobody knew wouldn't hurt although it was both hurting and haunting me every day. These struggles led me into a dark maze of dysfunction, where I became numb to my pain. It was my way of self-medicating, which ultimately led to an unwanted addiction that left me feeling miserable about my self-worth.

I know it may seem small to some people given the day and time we are in but as Pastor the weight of my decisions pulled at the worthiness of my call. Thus, the dysfunctional decisions made in times of disappointment became debilitating internally to both my confidence and my call. So as a pastor, my life lived on a cycle. I knew pornography was wrong, but I had become conditioned to it being the primary way of burying my struggles. Now, I know this may be weird reading this from a Pastor and somebody that you may admire but you will get over it. The truth is Even Pastors lose Hope.

Paul said in Romans 7:24 "O wretched man that I am! Who will deliver me from this body of death?" In other words, who can save a brother from himself? Disappointment started from just a distraction, and the duration of the situation transcended the offence of people in public to the offense of self in secret. Deep underneath a veil of secrecy was shame. While seemingly safe and private, this secrecy was a self-sabotaging mechanism that left my hope suffocating with guilt and gasping for breath. The rational response to my disappointment and frustration was to continue this cycle of self-defeat, all while others had high expectations of me. I set myself up for failure, like the pattern I'd experienced as a child, by expecting outcomes without fully considering the possibilities and realities of my situation. Understanding this process helps us navigate our emotional landscape, guiding us toward healing and renewal.

In the face of disappointment, it's easy to feel hope is slipping away, but that's when hope is most critical. The pain of unmet expectations can blind us to the possibilities still ahead, making us believe that failure defines us. Yet, hope is a quiet but powerful force that refuses to give up, even when everything seems lost. It invites us to shift our perspective—to see disappointment not as a dead end but a redirection toward something greater. Hope whispers that every setback is a setup for growth, resilience, and the eventual fulfillment of our deeper desires. By holding onto hope in moments of disappointment, we find the strength to keep moving forward, trusting that what's been delayed isn't denied. This chapter challenges us to dissect our disappointments, understanding them as part of the journey toward a stronger, more grounded hope that can withstand life's uncertainties

Overcoming disappointments does not require achieving perfection; instead, it involves recognizing that hope is present and available. The cure to disappointment is embracing the transformative power of hope. Hope is not about erasing our failures or attaining flawless outcomes. Instead, the beacon guides us through the darkness of disappointment, providing solace and strength. Proverbs 13:12 reminds us of that while "hope deferred makes the heart sick," a "desire fulfilled is a tree of life." This verse celebrates the profound beauty and resilience found in hope.

When we nurture hope, we open ourselves up to the possibility of growth, allowing our disappointments to become catalysts for healing and transformation. Hope doesn't just help us move forward—it lights the way, illuminating a path through our struggles and teaching us to find compassion for ourselves and others along the way. It empowers us to rise above life's challenges, whether from external letdowns or our own self-sabotage and gives us the strength to keep going. Hope reminds us that even in the face of failure, we can continue to evolve, rebuild, and pursue something better. It weaves resilience into the fabric of our lives, helping us find meaning in our hardships and a renewed sense of purpose as we push forward.

Chapter 5
DISCOURAGEMENT and DEPRESSION

"He who refuses to embrace a unique opportunity loses the prize as surely as if he had failed."

- African Proverb

Luke 24:24

"And certain of those who were with us went to the tomb and found it just as the women had said; but Him they did not see."

Hope can be fragile, like a small flame in the dark that can easily be blown out by discouragement and depression. When life brings disappointment after disappointment, it's like that flame gets weaker and weaker until it's barely there. Discouragement slowly creeps in, stealing our confidence and joy and making everything feel heavier. It's like someone slowly taking apart your spirit, piece by piece. If we don't deal with this discouragement, it can turn into deep depression, making us feel like there's nothing left to live for.

Think about those two men who once had a strong faith—they saw miracles and felt hope, but now all they could remember was a loss. It is a feeling many of us know too well. I've also been there, trying to encourage others while my hope was slipping away. I've faced times when everything felt like it was falling apart - losing a job, living out of my car, feeling completely lost. But even in those dark moments, I realized something important: hope isn't completely gone, even when it feels like it is. It's still there, waiting to be found again, even in the middle of our deepest despair.

Detours of Despair

The road felt like it would never end, each step getting heavier, like they were dragging the weight of their shattered dreams. These two guys, who used to be all about faith, now walked in silence, hearts hollowed out by the loss. This journey wasn't just about getting from one place to another—it was a painful walk through what was left of their hope. Every step was like pulling away from the spot where everything they believed was destroyed, a place that now felt empty and cold, where their once-lived life was just a memory.

Three days passed since their world fell apart, three days since they saw the light of their hope snuffed out on a cross. As they walked, they couldn't shake the whispers from that morning—the women talking about an empty tomb, saying they saw angels, claiming He was alive. But when they went to check it out, they found nothing. There were no signs, no answers—just emptiness, matching the hollowness inside them.

Each step they took was a desperate move to escape the crushing reality that everything they believed in was gone. The road they walked wasn't just pavement—it was a mirror, showing them the downward spiral into the depths of their despair. With every step, they left behind the last fragile bits of their faith, looking for peace in the only place that seemed to offer it: despair.

Hitting Rock Bottom
My story isn't one of endless gloom and doom, but I need to take you into my darkest moments to understand it truly. In those times of deep despair—when you feel surrounded by people yet utterly alone—the need for hope is most profound. When you're feeling broken, empty, and overlooked, this is when hope matters most.

Hope, sometimes so vibrant, can be fragile. It's like a candle in a storm, flickering in the face of discouragement and depression. The slightest gust of doubt can threaten to snuff it out. When disappointments pile up, that once-bright light begins to fade, casting shadows where hope used to shine. And from those shadows, discouragement creeps in, slowly draining the light from our lives and leaving us feeling suffocated and lost.

The autopsy of hope doesn't end with discouragement—it goes deeper, examining the gravity of rock-bottom depression that often follows. When hope fades and discouragement takes hold, it can lead us down a dark path.

First, discouragement settles in like a slow poison, eroding our confidence and enthusiasm. Then, depression begins to take root, pulling us further into despair and making it harder to see any light at the end of the tunnel. Finally, as depression deepens, it can trigger destructive behaviors. These actions, born out of hopelessness, can push us away from the things that once brought us comfort and strength. In this downward spiral, we find ourselves caught in a cycle where each step leads to a darker place, making it seem like there's no way out.

The Prison of Hopelessness

There was a time when I used to preach to inmates in a federal prison in Petersburg, VA. I saw it in their eyes—potential lost, dreams crushed, promises that slipped away. I talked about hope, but their stories were filled with regret. "If only I knew then what I know now," they'd say. But life doesn't give you that kind of mercy. It traps you in crisis; without Christ, hope feels as far away as freedom.

Discouragement will imprison anyone if it lingers too long. It locks you in a cell of pity with no apparent way out. That was my reality in 2020. I was in my mid-thirties, a youth pastor who had lost all passion. I was stuck in a cycle of comparing myself to others, watching my peers speed ahead while I felt like I was slowly sinking into quicksand. I hated my life. I was a prisoner to a paycheck, trying to inspire others to pray when I couldn't even find the strength to pray myself.

Then the pandemic hit. The whole world shut down, and I barely kept the church alive. The stress was killing me, draining me dry. I'll never forget the day my mom called, screaming that my aunt had died in her sleep. I was live-streaming a service, and like always, I did what I'd been trained to do—I took a deep breath, sucked it up, and kept going. But inside, I was falling apart.

I'd just been rejected from a doctoral program. I felt trapped in a dead-end job, and now, my grandmother's only sister—my only biological aunt on my mom's side—was gone, just like that. I was discouraged. I flew home, faced the grief, and stood at my aunt's funeral, broken. As I broke down, a family member whispered, "You're supposed to be a preacher." Those words cut deep. I had to keep my pain locked inside, but the more I pushed it down, the more it pushed back.

When I got back to D.C., I wanted out. I'd spent my whole life running from anything challenging. Conflict scared me, so I'd keep moving, processing things my way. But I hit a point where I was just tired and overwhelmed. There is a feeling of being agitated and irritable at the slightest thing. So, I decided to do what I always did in hard times Leave. I packed up and moved back to Chicago, hoping things would get better. But they didn't. Things got worse. My family was falling apart, the community was a mess, and my life was ultimately upside down. For three years, I drifted through the city I loved, discouraged, and depressed. I heard the cries of grieving mothers, felt the anger of traumatized teenagers, and saw the heavy cloud of hopelessness that hung over generations. I was backed into a corner, and I felt hopeless.

I know it's expected that I'll wrap this chapter up with a positive spin, but that's not how it went down. Sometimes, life must unravel before it can start making sense completely. During this time, I put all my trust in a church leader I believed in, someone I thought had my back, like Batman and Robin. But out of nowhere, I got called into the office and fired unexpectedly—just like that. It was a gut punch that knocked the wind out of me. I didn't know how to make it for the next three months. I was broken and I was in crisis. I was living out of my car, bouncing from one hotel to the next. The stress was so heavy that I'd wake up and find my hair shedding on the pillow, falling out from the pressure of this mental prison.

Kill, Steal, and Destroy

One of the greatest tools of the enemy is the spirit of discouragement. It's a trap that causes believers to become so disillusioned with their problems that they forget about their promises. The prison of discouragement is where a ruthless force aims to kill, steal, and destroy. It comes at your darkest moment to suffocate hope and rob us of our vitality. The statistics paint a grim picture: suicide rates among young people have skyrocketed in recent years, with nearly 15% of high school students in the U.S. seriously considering it, according to recent surveys. Discouragement twists the mind, making life seem unbearable and leading to these devastating outcomes. It steals our motivation, eroding our confidence and pushing us toward isolation. The loss of self-esteem and purpose caused by persistent discouragement often leads to destructive behaviors, such as substance abuse and self-harm, as individuals try to cope with their overwhelming despair. Psychologically, discouragement acts like a thief, taking away our dreams and ambitions and leaving behind a barren landscape of rusted prison bars, unfulfilled potential, and shattered lives.

In the autopsy of my life, the signs of my self-destruction were unmistakable. I neglected my prayer life, lost focus, and existed in a constant state of numbness. My sleep became endless, my health deteriorated, and I turned to destructive habits. Each symptom was a stark indicator of the deep-rooted sickness called discouragement. It wasn't just a rough patch; it was a full-blown crisis. I was spiraling into a cycle of self-destruction, where every unhealthy choice and every avoided conflict contributed to my downfall.

I spent years running from anything that threatened to make me face my pain or vulnerability. I avoided confronting my fears and struggles, thinking that if I just kept moving, I'd find relief. But eventually, I reached a point where there was no more room to escape. My life hit rock bottom, and in that dark, unrelenting space, I was forced to confront the truth of my situation and surrender. In this profound moment of loss and facing my own despair, I uncovered what I had been missing all along—a deeper understanding of myself and the hope I thought was gone.

Autopsy of the Soul

The disciples of Christ had seen miracles, witnessed movements, and felt the pulse of something greater. But in this moment, all they could remember was death. The Autopsy of Hope continues, examining the fatal wounds inflicted by discouragement. It's the final stage of hope's death, where nothing seems worse than the hollow emptiness of a discouraged heart.

Hopeless people resort to any means to survive. Like a person drowning requiring a lifeguard but whose fear has frustrated the mission of saving. The Lifeguard can lose their life trying to save a person that panics out of control. This is Discouragement. It creeps into the mind, eroding confidence and enthusiasm, chipping away at the very core of who we are. It's like a slow autopsy on our soul, cutting away at our courage, layer by layer.

When we experience failure after failure, it feels like the world is wielding a chisel, carving away our self-esteem. Each blow leaves a scar, reminding us of where we've fallen short. The vision of a hopeful future blurs until it fades into nothingness, leaving only discontentment and despair. The distance created by disappointment causes one to dwell in the perception of defeat, and nothing or no one can convince otherwise concerning the weight of the situation.

Discouragement doesn't always show its face. It's a master of disguise, hiding behind forced smiles and hollow laughter. We see it in the statistics—suicide rates climbing among young Black teenagers in America, their inner battles invisible to the outside world. Discouragement left unchecked spirals into depression. It whispers lies, convincing us that there's nothing left to live for, nothing worth waking up to.

Buried Alive, but I Survived

Hope is fragile, making this an autopsy of the most challenging kind: discouragement, depression, and destructive behavior. Each stage reveals how these elements affect our emotional and psychological well-being, often blocking even the faintest glimmers of hope.– Emotionally and mentally, it creates a gap between our aspirations and perceived capabilities. It fosters a sense of inadequacy that diminishes our will to strive and thrive. It's an erosion that manifests in our daily lives, making manageable tasks monumental obstacles. Depression feeds a loop of negative self-talk and stagnation, isolating us from opportunities and support.

As we sink deeper, depression becomes a profound abyss where discouragement evolves into a pervasive heaviness. Depression often feels like a physical weight, making even the most straightforward actions seem insurmountable. I'm all too familiar with the enduring numbness. Relationships become frayed as isolation deepens. Depression transforms potential into paralysis, casting a long shadow over our ability to grow and fulfill our potential.

Destructive behavior emerges as the final stage, where despair manifests through actions undermining our well-being and future. It becomes a form of self-sabotage that accelerates the cycle of hopelessness. Destructive behavior is an attempt to regain control in a situation where everything feels uncontrollable. It's a cry for help, albeit through harmful means—a series of daily consequences compound, further damaging relationships and eroding self-worth. The destructive spiral creates a seemingly inescapable vortex of despair. Depression is more than a mood or an emotion, it is the psychological reality of simply hitting rock bottom. It screams "I've had enough".

Dr. King said, "Riots is the language of the unheard." I recall the year 2016, while in Washington, DC, we became aware of a murder case of Freddie Gray in Baltimore, MD. This was the period of great exposure regarding the treatment of African Americans at the hands of police. Some cases showed that individuals who resisted and complied met the same fatal fate. As a result, the community lost hope, and their response was a riot. The people grew tired of the same story with the same outcome. There was no more energy to march and sing; something had to be done, even if what was done was criminal. The streets were burning, stores were destroyed and boarded, and security was breached with every man for themselves.

There comes a time when we become exhausted by unfulfilled expectations, broken promises, and economic inequality. Broken trust knocks the wind and energy out of your belief system, causing you to rest and reflect. Left to our mind, based upon the distance you have taken to get to the place that you are in, space is dangerous and requires help. In this space, I realized beyond church, titles, and preaching that I not only needed help, but I was desperate for hope.

Yet, even in these profound depths, a flicker of hope remains—a testament to the resilience of the human spirit. I have seen this firsthand in inner-city environments steeped in hopelessness. Individuals and communities have risen with remarkable strength from these ashes, demonstrating that greatness can emerge. Inner-city youth who face pervasive violence and economic hardship often rise to become leaders, innovators, and advocates. Historical figures like Nelson Mandela and Malala Yousafzai, who emerged from intense adversity, used their experiences to inspire global change, proving that greatness can stem from hopelessness.

Rising from the Ashes

In the center of your crisis, there is always a way to see Christ—the anchor of your hope. Hope becomes a guiding beacon, showing us that something vital remains even when everything seems lost. We must fight the distance that discouragement creates. I was incarcerated in the prison of depression, distant from everyone and everything. But in that dark place, I realized something: I wasn't dead which meant I wasn't done. Let me rewrite so that so that you can read it out loud to yourself...You're not dead which means You're not Done!

Even while buried in the depths of despair, hope is still alive. In the core of your crisis, Christ is always present. The Autopsy of Hope isn't merely about examining what's dead—it's ultimately about discovering what's alive. Hope isn't always easy to grasp, but it exists, even when all seems lost. It lies in the ashes of our disappointments, waiting to be reborn. Although it may appear that everything is on pause Hope still has a pulse.

Chapter 6
DISCOVERY CHANNEL

It is better to build a house and invite everyone in than to build a wall and keep everyone out."

– African Proverb

Luke 24:30-31

Now it came to pass, as He sat at the table with them, that He took bread, blessed and broke it, and gave it to them. Then their eyes were opened and they knew Him; and He vanished from their sight.

Identifying the problem is like the first incision in an autopsy—necessary yet insufficient. It's the initial step, the moment the scalpel touches the surface, but uncovering the root cause requires more than just making that first cut. Walking in the promise, however, demands the kind of deep, relentless probing that comes only through the dissection of despair and the meticulous examination of our innermost wounds.

This chapter is difficult to embody. It goes beyond diagnosis, beyond identifying problems, and beyond the description of any crisis. Discovery is about finding solutions. Discovery, especially the discovery of hope, often begins in the darkest chambers of crisis, where light seems absent, and every breath feels like a battle.

In these moments, where the lifelessness of hope seems inevitable, we must dig deeper. We must peel back the layers of doubt, fear, and despair, like a forensic pathologist examining tissue and bone to uncover the truth. The truth is that hope has not died—it is hidden, obscured by the decay of unmet expectations and the root of deferred dreams. In these moments, when everything around us seems to be decomposing, we must remember, recognize, and reclaim the power of hope.

We must scrutinize every aspect of our pain, dissect it, and search within the wreckage for the remaining fragments of hope. Like a skilled examiner, we must be thorough, stubborn, and unyielding in our search for answers, for the power of hope is often buried beneath the surface, waiting to be resurrected.

In the sterile, cold chambers of crisis, where the weight of despair threatens to suffocate us, hope must be rediscovered, not as a distant possibility, but as a vital organ essential for survival. We must reclaim it, piece by piece, stitch by stitch, until it is restored to its rightful place at the core of our being. A self-examination is necessary to rise from the ashes of our darkest moments, and the admission that You need Hope.

Remember, Recognize, and Reclaim It
In Luke 24:30, when they entered the house with Jesus, something miraculous happened—their eyes were opened, and they saw Him for who He truly was. This moment of revelation was profound, but it was fleeting. As soon as they recognized Him, He vanished from their sight. It's a poignant reminder that moments of clarity, those brief glimpses of hope and truth, can often feel like they slip away just as quickly as they come. Simply put Hope is only based on what is not seen.

In this life, you will have trouble, experience unwanted challenges, loved ones will die, relationships will fail, and hope will always remain the unseen compass navigating us beyond every vanishing victory. The disappearance of Jesus did not diminish the significance of what they had just experienced. Instead, it cemented a more profound understanding, a lasting imprint on their souls that the hope He represented was still alive even in His absence.

This encounter speaks to the nature of discovery in our own lives. We often find ourselves in dark places, yearning for answers, searching for hope, only to have it appear for a moment before it seems to disappear again. Romans 8:24 states "Hope that is seen is not hope at all" emphasizes that hope is inherently tied to the unseen and the yet-to-come.
If we already possess or see something, there's no need to hope for it. Hope is about trusting and believing in things that have not yet materialized or been fully realized. Remember it's what can be confidently expected. It's about looking forward to what lies ahead, with faith that it will come to pass, even when there's no tangible evidence or assurance in the present moment. Hope is a forward-looking virtue. It requires us to look beyond our current circumstances and hold on to the belief in possibilities and promises that have yet to be fulfilled.

Hope emerges whenever death looms as a possibility. It is the force that keeps dreams alive, propels people through pain, and sustains us in the face of despair. Hope is a lifeline amid life's most significant trials, including death. Picture life as a complex body, where each challenge is a crucial part that must be carefully examined. The Autopsy of Hope shows that hope has hidden strengths; it endures beyond death, navigates challenges, and guides us through even the darkest times.

Like the disciples, we must hold onto the truth. Even when hope feels distant and vanishes from our immediate grasp, the memory of its presence remains, guiding us forward. It is the essence of discovery—not just seeing with our eyes but understanding with our hearts, knowing that what we experienced was legit, and though sometimes elusive, is always within reach if we remember, recognize, and reclaim it.

Adjusting Vision and Rising Strong

My frequent grammatical errors in college led my professor to recommend an eye exam. The doctor fitted me with new lenses, and suddenly, everything came into sharp focus. What had seemed missing was present all along. This experience taught me that, like vision, hope requires continual adjustment. The discovery of hope requires a channel to intentional focus. You must find hope even when you don't feel as if it is present.

Life can drag us into dark and difficult places, but hope persists like a constant pulse amid chaos. Despite despair, depression, defeat, and darkness, something profound can rise from the depths.

Just as my vision needed adjustment, so does hope require realignment. Rocky movies capture this journey perfectly. They show how every knockdown can lead to a comeback. When knocked down, hope becomes our reason to rise, cling to our dreams, and rediscover our strength. Our initial version of hope may need to be tested and broken, but true victory emerges through the One who offers genuine hope.

Our pain has purpose and direction. Hope helps us navigate hurt, maneuver around obstacles, and keep our heads high when failure tries to redefine our finish line.

Like Rocky, who rose from every fall, our trials reveal our profound resilience. Each challenge is like a new round to fight for life. Hope is our trainer pushing us to dig deeper and stand taller. Just as Rocky faced defeat only to return stronger, our greatest strength is the relentless pursuit of hope. Through every battle, as we get knocked down and rise again, each testimony uncovers the unbreakable tenacity of hope.

Where Hope Thrives

In the dead of winter 2021, I rented a U-Haul, and with the help of two friends, my mission was to escape Washington, DC. After 18 long years, I was fed up with ministry. I no longer wanted to preach; I was drained and desperate for a change. Like the followers I was running away because of my disappointment. With snow swirling around us, I packed up my life and headed to Chicago, hoping for a fresh start.

Chicago welcomed me with open arms and freezing temperatures. I became an outreach director, serving the underserved. Yet, despite my new role, a nagging emptiness remained. The city felt alien. Old hangouts were gone, friends and family had moved on, and the rising crime made it feel unsafe. I felt lost.

Then came a night that changed everything in 2022. Scrolling through Instagram, I saw a shocking video of a teenager, Seandell Holiday, being shot downtown. The cold indifference of the crowd struck me deeply. I was furious and heartbroken. I contacted local mentors, to discover ways to help the grieving family. Unexpectedly, they needed a preacher for the funeral. It was the crisis I had vowed to avoid, yet it demanded more than words. It demanded hope.

Standing before hundreds of young people, including the Mayor of Chicago, I preached through the tears. I spoke to teenagers who were preparing for yet another funeral. It wasn't just sorrow; it was a stark revelation. I felt the burden of conviction to reveal to an upcoming generation what was clearly unknown. Hope wasn't just an emotion but a substance that separated the living from the dying. In that moment of despair, I discovered hope within myself which is to be hope for someone else.

The first year in Chicago was tough. I woke up daily searching for what no longer existed. Raised in the city I left for college at 17, I expected to pick up where I left off. Instead, I found myself discontent as an Outreach Director, but I learned that hope thrives where needed most.

The Anatomy of Hope

When Jesus' friend Lazarus fell ill, Jesus waited until Lazarus died before arriving. Jesus wasn't distracted by what seemed lifeless. It wasn't indifference; it was intentional. Sometimes, what we hope for doesn't happen on our terms or timelines and our desires go unmet. But often, these endings make room for something new.

In life's autopsy, you can't reach your destiny without first confronting a crisis. Hopelessness is the cold hand of fear, but hope is the warm pulse that fights back. Hope reveals itself when you least expect it. Lazarus' family had the funeral and the burial before Jesus arrived. Yet, even the grave was not strong enough to stop Hope from getting Lazarus up and calling him out. I don't know how long your dream, vision, idea has been buried under the debris of depression but this book is written to convince you that it will come alive again.

In the context of an autopsy, "discovery" refers to uncovering and identifying the underlying causes of death. It involves a detailed examination of the body, organs, tissues, and sometimes external circumstances to reveal what may not be immediately visible. This process often leads to discovering previously unknown or hidden conditions, injuries, or diseases that contributed to or caused the death.

Through careful investigation and analysis, the pathologist can piece together the puzzle of what happened, shedding light on the reasons behind the death. Do you remember why your dreams died? Why did your marriage fail? Why did you give up on things that mattered to you? Digging for the answers to life's most challenging questions is what "Discovery" is all about. His disappearance didn't erase their hope; it anchored it. The memory of hope must stay alive, even when the moment is gone.

The easiest way to discover true Hope is to surrender. Hope is the "I can," the "I will," and the "I am" within us. When the disciples saw Jesus, it reignited their hope, showing them that belief alone can sustain us through anything. Life's challenges don't have a one-size-fits-all solution, but often, something must end for something new to begin. You can either let life change you or choose to change your life—hope distinguishes the perspectives of both paths, whether you keep going or give up.

A New Perspective

In 2023, I traveled to South Africa through a study abroad program focused on clinical counseling and trauma precisely because the Seandell Holiday crisis moved me. The journey was more than just academic; it was a profound lesson in resilience and the power of perspective. Walking through the streets of Soweto, I saw firsthand the remnants of apartheid but also the unyielding spirit of its people. I heard of their direct experience with the atrocities of apartheid. The stark contrast between the beauty of the land and the harsh realities its people endured struck me deeply. After over 30 years of trauma and trials their songs were still drenched in the hope that was greater than anyone could comprehend.

Nelson Mandela's life, etched into the very fabric of this nation, revealed hope in a way I had never fully understood. His decades of suffering in a prison cell, stripped of freedom yet never of dignity, pushed me to see hope in a new light. Mandela didn't just survive; he transformed his pain into a beacon of hope for millions. If impoverished children in Africa can hold onto hope without justice or reparation, then surely, I can and surely you will.

I realized that hope isn't always found in grand gestures or perfect circumstances. It can be discovered in the quiet strength of those who endure the unimaginable. Mandela's life is a modern testament to this discovery. For others, it might be a local teacher, preacher, or friend. Hope can easily slip through our fingers if our focus is on material things rather than the deeper purpose hope serves.

We believe, so we think; we think, so we speak; and we speak hope until it manifests. There are days when I look into the eyes of people who expect greatness from me, and it feels like I'm on a seesaw, balancing hope, and doubt. Yet, this season, I am not panicking, running away, or self-destructing. I draw strength from every moment hope proved helpful in my past, proving that God has a plan for my life. And so, I remain hopeful and convinced that Better is Coming.

Life is a series of rediscovering hope – again and again and again. Each victory and defeat lay the foundation for our next encounter with hope. We will always need hope because life's challenges are relentless. As we move forward, we must remember that discovering hope is not enough. It's not a one-time event—it's a lifelong journey. It is the fuel that powers our faith, the anchor that holds us steady, and the light that guides us through the darkest times.

Hope Remains

A morbid title, "Autopsy of Hope," but so many people walk away from faith and churches because they have no hope. There is often a lot of emphasis on Faith which presumes that an induvial already has Hope. But, in this climate of distress and despair there is a need to remind even believers that there is still Hope. Hope comes from dead places—from things unseen. I believe that until you are willing to allow your pre-existing goals to die you will continue to experience the cycle of disappointment.

So, you must determine to see a realistic picture of your life, and make a decision to receive Christ, to which only hope can be discovered. God used death, doubt, discouragement, despair, and depression to bring me to my knees. Amid the darkness, there will always be light within and that shining glare is not emotion but it's expectation and its Hope. Therefore, the journey and route to discover this hope was necessary and nothing has been wasted.

Though delicate and vulnerable, hope possesses extraordinary resilience that defies the odds. It is like a muscle—one that must be exercised, stretched, and strained to grow stronger. In the face of overwhelming darkness, when it feels as if the world is collapsing around you, hope demands that you push through the pain and dig deeper into the marrow of your being to find the strength to carry on.

However, hope is more than just an inner force; it is contagious, spreading like a lifeline to those around you. Those who cling to hope are not consumed by despair—they are anchored by it, grounded in something far more significant than themselves. The remedy to their suffering lies in the profound realization that hope is not a theory but it is truth. Hope is a living, breathing presence. It is not just an idea; it is embodied in the essence of the One who offers it, inviting us to hold fast and never let go. Hope has a name and it is Jesus!

Chapter 7

DEMONSTRATION HOPE

"The best time to plant a tree was 20 years ago. The second-best time is now."

– African Proverb

Luke 24:32

And they said to one another, "Did not our heart burn within us while He talked with us on the road, and while He opened the Scriptures to us?" So, they rose up that very hour and returned to Jerusalem

Throughout the seven chapters of this book, our journey parallels the seven miles the two disciples walked on the road to Emmaus. Just as they despaired, believing hope had died with Jesus in Jerusalem, we, too, explore the depths where hope seemed lost. This book serves as our autopsy of hope, revealing that even when dreams and ambitions appear dead, hope remains alive, resurrecting and renewing the beliefs of those who dare to embrace it.

In Luke 24:33, they return to Jerusalem and report, "It is true! The Lord has risen." This highlights the transformation that transpired from doubt and disappointment to belief and joy, illustrating the power of recognizing hope even in moments of despair. Notice there wasn't any singing, or praise breaks there was just revelation of the man that they thought was dead being now alive. This signified that Hope was stronger than even death.

True hope offers a divine demonstration. It demands action. Without action, hope is only a dream—a mere whisper in the wind. Hope is more than a wish. When hope stirs within us, it ignites a fire that cannot be extinguished. It pushes us from the shadows of doubt into the light of certainty.

Dr. Martin Luther King Jr. once said, "There comes a time when silence is no longer necessary." This is the time for hope to be loud and clear. We must demonstrate hope. Silence is no longer an option. Purpose is calling, and people are waiting. Political divides tear the world apart. The economy has raised the cost of gas and groceries, crime and violence have filled our streets, and it's clear that something is missing within the emerging generation. What separates the history maker from those who follow history are those who dared to demonstrate hope amid the crisis and dream above the odds.

From Silence to Action

Hope rises in the depths of despair when the world seems to crumble. It calls us to move, act, stand up, and be counted. The exact moment that Jesus ate with them is when they realized that for the entire time of their journey, He was alive. In other words, though they left Jerusalem with no hope, hope never left them. The revelation of Jesus provoked a hope that was reborn within them. This realization didn't just comfort them—it provoked them to act.

Hope provoked them to confront what they once feared; instead of staying in Emmaus, they returned to the place where hope was discovered. They rushed back to Jerusalem with a simple yet profound message: "He's alive." Hope revives and reminds us that we are not alone. It creates the courage to obey God—the confidence to rest in the reality that God's got us. Hope is the believer's superpower. It transforms our fear into fuel, and coverts our despair into determination.

The Leap of Faith

I remember my 30th birthday when I went skydiving. Although I looked courageous on the outside, I was terrified inside. Skydiving is an intense confrontation with fear, requiring immense courage to overcome. It challenges our primal fear of falling, the unknown, and potential equipment failure, all of which can be paralyzing.

To face these fears, skydivers must summon the courage to trust—trust in the equipment, the training, and the instructors. This courage also involves letting go of control and embracing vulnerability, as jumping is a literal and metaphorical surrender. Ultimately, skydiving demands the bravery to embrace the unknown, leading to a liberating and empowering experience that defies fear and elevates the spirit.

As I stood at the edge of the airplane door, anxiety tightened its grip, threatening to paralyze me. But with every heartbeat, I felt the steady presence of the experienced jumper strapped to my back, his calm assurance cutting through my fear. His confidence became my lifeline, and in that moment of terror and trust, I found the courage to leap into the void. And so, I jumped—letting go of fear and embracing the unknown.

Hope tells you, despite the fear, despite the circumstances, to jump anyway. The leap of faith is not about the absence of fear; it's about moving forward despite your heart beating violently against your ribcage.

Faith's Heartbeat

Hope is the heartbeat of faith. Hope keeps faith alive, even when all seems lost. You can have hope without faith, but you cannot have faith without hope. Once filled with fear, the disciples found their courage through the resurrected Christ to become obedient at spreading the message to all people that the man who once died is alive. Jesus no longer had to be physically present for their hope to be potent. The mere presentation that He had risen was evidence enough.

When hope is demonstrated, it burns brighter than any fear. It turns fear into fire—fueling our journey through the darkest valleys. When you take action with hope, you don't just face your fears—you turn them into fuel. Instead of letting fear and other excuses hold you back, use it to propel yourself forward. Hope isn't passive; it's a powerful force that, when activated, burns through the obstacles in your path. In those moments when the darkness seems overwhelming, hope lights the way, guiding us with a fierce determination to keep moving. When this hope happens, you will experience a demonstration.

A Spiritual Autopsy

I've laid bare my soul in this book, dissecting my journey of hope and despair. I've shown how placing hope in anything temporal, leads to spiritual decay. Like an autopsy, where we examine the cause of death, I've peeled back the layers of my own life to reveal the moments when worldly hype masqueraded as hope, only to lead to disappointment. The idea of writing this book came to me over ten years ago, and at first, my heart beat with hope. I was passionate about the message and the potential of motivating a generation to become agents of change. But as time passed, life's scalpel carved away at my ambition, turning it into anxiety.

In December 2023, I found myself lying on the cold slab of life's reality. Yet, during that season of crisis, I discovered something crucial during this autopsy: I had to follow the favor. I had to trace back the origins of true hope, not the counterfeit hope that the world offers that fails to produce results.

At this moment, I realized that hope without God is mere hype—a hollow promise without guarantees. It wasn't until I returned to D.C., where I first encountered true hope, that I understood this critical difference. Just as an autopsy reveals what lies beneath the surface, I came to see that true hope is never about what we see; it's about confidently trusting in the unseen promises of God.

Follow the Favor

Hope isn't just for moments of triumph; it's for the times when life feels like a morgue, cold and lifeless. I've discovered that hope is not just for the good times. It's for the hard times, the crisis moments, the times when nothing seems to make sense. Following the favor means trusting the path within in God's promises.

The unique thing about the path is that it's a clear picture with limited details on how to get there. Even when the path is obscured by darkness and doubt you have hold on to your hope. Psalm 42:5 "Why art thou cast down, O my soul? And why art thou disquieted within me? Hope thou in God." Hope without God is like a body without a soul—empty and lifeless. Hope without God is only hype.

When I say, "Hope without God is only hype," I mean that hope, without a solid spiritual foundation, becomes nothing more than empty promises. It's like a dazzling facade that looks appealing but fails to deliver meaningful results. Without grounding in something greater, hope can end up as an empty wish or unrealistic expectations. But hope with God is a force that can resurrect the dead, breathe life into the hopeless, and change the world. It's a hope based on God's promises, which are reliable and trustworthy, not just wishful thinking or false promises.

Birthing the Impossible

Abraham's hope profoundly impacted the world. His legacy continues to serve as a beacon of resilience and faith, demonstrating that one person's unwavering trust in a promise can ripple through time and inspire transformative change across the globe.

Abraham's story teaches us how hope can achieve the seemingly impossible. Imagine being 100 years old, with your spouse at 90, and being told you will become parents. This promise seemed impossible due to their advanced age and the natural impossibility of conception at such an age. It sounds unbelievable, even absurd. Yet, Abraham held onto hope despite the odds. It wasn't wishful thinking but a profound belief in a promise-defying logic.

For twenty long years, Abraham and Sarah waited. Their journey was marked by patience and persistence, holding onto hope when reality seemed harsh and unkind. Romans 4:18 captures this beautifully: "Against all hope, Abraham in hope believed." Their hope wasn't a fleeting dream but a powerful force transforming their lives.

When the promise finally came to pass, Sarah experienced the physical and emotional pain of childbirth at 90 years old. Demonstrating hope is not easy. It was not just a matter of physical discomfort but a profound struggle against the natural limitations of her body and the societal expectations of her time. The pain and effort of childbirth at such an age added a significant layer of difficulty to their journey, highlighting the miraculous nature of their son Isaac's birth.

Despite these challenges, their faith in God's promise was ultimately rewarded. Sometimes the promise of God requires your participation. Isaac's birth was pivotal, transforming their struggle into a legacy that would influence generations. Abraham became the father of many nations. His hope demonstrates how enduring faith and patience can lead to extraordinary outcomes. When one person dares to hold onto hope, they can inspire and bring about profound transformation.

A Legacy of Hope
Hope isn't just for us—it's for those who follow. When the disciples returned to Jerusalem, they were not only bearing the message of Christ's resurrection for themselves. They were carrying hope for generations to come. Their demonstration of hope was not just a personal triumph but a legacy.

We, too, are called to leave a legacy of hope. Our actions today can inspire faith in those who come after us. The demonstration of hope is the inheritance we pass down. The disciples faced a reality that had not changed—the same oppressive government and the same life-and-death dangers. Yet, the circumstances did not diminish their hope. Instead, it grew stronger. When Jesus disappeared, they were no longer sad. They had learned to trust in the unseen.

What is the point of hope if it only exists in our imagination? Hope must come alive in You. Hope must manifest in our lives, even amid crisis. It is in these moments that hope proves its power.

The Power of Hope

Hope's true power emerges in the daunting depths of our darkest valleys—where the climb seems impossible. Fatherlessness, poverty, and societal stigmas can shackle us to our circumstances, painting a bleak picture of our potential. Yet hope ignites a fierce defiance against these limitations. It stirs us to rise above, to break free from the bonds of our birthright burdens, and to showcase that our circumstances do not confine us.

Hope is our steadfast anchor when everything else falters. Hope in God is our unyielding foundation in a constantly crumbling world. While everything else might disappoint, hope remains our unwavering truth. It's not merely a fleeting dream but a reliable refuge.

Abraham's hope defied logic and natural limitations. It wasn't rooted in what was visible or plausible but anchored deeply in

God's promises. This profound trust ensured that his hope never faltered or failed him.

Ambition, unanchored from hope, can swiftly devolve into debilitating anxiety. I learned this the hard way, as my delay in writing this book made me doubt the essence of hope. But divine hope stands resilient and unfailing. It's not a mirage but a beacon that never disappoints.

Romans 5:3-4a declares, "We glory in our sufferings because we know that suffering produces perseverance; perseverance, character; and character, hope. And Hope makes us not ashamed". Hope will never play You. Hope is not wishful thinking; it's potent, transforming trials into triumphs. It never leaves us in shame but builds us into beacons of belief.

Hope in Action

In 2016, we struggled with the fragments of Obama's audacity of hope in a system that has proven to be divided and dysfunctional. Personally, both sides of the political aisle had proven that they prefer their party over the people. So, we have to learn from the Past to Progress in the Present to be Productive in the future. Today, the same individual who ran against then Hillary Clinton is contending with our first black Vice President in the run for Presidency. It's still amazing to believe that after 8 long years, we are still facing similar challenges. But, hope in any political party or leader outside of Christ is wasted energy and expectation.

It has been proven to fail and leave us unfulfilled every time. Our hope must remain in Christ.

Romans 15:13 states "May the God of hope fill you with all joy and peace in believing, so that by the power of the Holy Spirit you may abound in hope." My grandmother used to sing the song "build your hopes on things eternal, Hold to God's unchanging Hand." Hope is a lifetime activity. Every crisis we face becomes a catalyst for transformation, propelling us to instigate meaningful change. This change is an abstract concept and the tangible embodiment of hope actively at work. When we confront and overcome challenges, we turn hope from a mere idea into a visible force driving progress. Each time we face adversity and choose to act, we transform hope into a powerful demonstration of resilience and possibility.

Change, therefore, becomes the living proof of hope's effectiveness, illustrating how hope, when put into action, can reshape our circumstances and lead to profound, lasting impact. Through our responses to crises, we manifest hope's true potential, showing that the pursuit of change fueled by hope can illuminate the path to a brighter future, even in the darkest times.

So, as Jesse Jackson once said, "Keep hope alive." When times are rough, keep hope alive. When you feel that you can't make it, keep hope alive. When it seems like everything is lost, keep hope alive. Trust that you will not fail when your anchor in hope is God. One of my favorite stories in the Bible is 2 Kings 7. Two men who were abandoned outside the city gates and plagued with a skin disease spoke with each other about their life decisions. They ask each other, "Should we sit here until we die"? Hope caused them not to settle and take a risk. So, they decided not to wait any longer but to risk it all in the conviction that at least they tried. When you realize who holds the future, today's problems will never be a concern.

Spreading Hope without Hype

Hope is not meant to sit idle or dormant. It is intended to be shared, demonstrated, and lived out. Maybe you are on the fence reading this and, like the disciples, are gripped with the fear of the unknown. Perhaps life has been so complicated that you have lost the energy to trust again. But I'm on an assignment to tell you to Try hope again. Take a moment to breathe: inhale and exhale. This is the most critical season in your life, and everything you do now will reflect how you live later. So, today is the day. It's time to start over, apply, start your business plan, write your book, meet someone new, start praying, and begin daily devotions. Whatever you do, you have to keep moving forward and believe again. Your belief will provoke your behavior. Hope is alive, and it calls us to action.

Hope and hype are two different realities. When Jesus was dead the same government was in power, yet the disciples still held on to hope. Hope caused them to birth change where there was crisis. Hype feels good, but hope can hurt. Hype vanishes, but hope endures. Hype often disappoints, but hope sustains. Hype promises instant results, but hope requires patience. Hype can manipulate, but hope can motivate.

The legitimacy of hope can be compared to an expectant mother at the end of her last trimester. There are a variety of questions and concerns that may arise regarding the baby that she is carrying. However, one thing that can never be debated is that every pregnancy has an expected delivery. Such is life; many have felt the contractions of death, doubt, disappointment, discouragement, and even depression. It has felt like a never-ending cycle of defeat. Yet, the strength of your contraction only reveals how close you are to birth everything you expect to produce.

Relax. You are closer than you realize and doing better than you can imagine. The two primary ingredients to hope are Breath and Belief; with those features, you can confront any crisis and allow the pressure to push out the change you have been destined to produce. Nothing can be done without hope. Hope shifts you from simply existing to being effective. What separates the good from the great? Hope.

As I examine everything I have experienced in my lifetime, real hope causes me to be grateful for everything. I realized the crisis was created so that I didn't settle. The hope I had in people, places, and things was fragile and always failed. Yet, it was at my lowest that I had no other option but to look up, and when I looked up, God looked out.

Every chapter that I experienced was a contraction necessary to my birthing experience. Without the pain of the crisis, this book would have never been written, and you or your life would have never been transformed through these words. So, thank God for equipping us and instilling the indestructible power of hope within our DNA.

You are the testament of Hope. Hope doesn't focus on survival, but hope is about rising. Maya Angelou wrote a famous poem titled Still I Rise. One of the strongest lines from the poem "Still I Rise" is "Bringing the gifts that my ancestors gave, I am the dream and the hope of the slave. I rise, I rise, I rise." By the time you finish reading this book, you will no longer need an autopsy in any area of your life. Hope is alive. Now that hope has resurrected your dead dreams and paralyzing disappointments. You have an obligation to spread the message. The good news of Hope gives people a reason to believe again in something greater than themselves.

As you finish this book, let the resurrection of your hope set off a spark that ignites others. Your journey isn't just about personal renewal—it's a call to action, urging others to rise above doubt, disappointment, and discouragement. In the midst of crisis, you're not here merely to survive but to birth real change, to become the force of transformation when hope seems out of reach. Armed with this renewed hope, you have the power to uplift those around you and prove that as long as Jesus is alive, hope will never die. Today is the day for hope to be reborn—right here, right now. The world is waiting for you to step into your purpose and become the catalyst for something greater. Don't make us wait any longer. Go out there and show the world what hope in action looks like! So, in the words of Your boy Pastor Will, Make Hope Dope Again!

FINAL THOUGHT FROM THE AUTHOR

In The Autopsy of Hope: Birthing Change in Crisis, we've uncovered how hope, even when lost, can be reborn through surrender—letting go and trusting in something greater than ourselves. For Black boys and girls, growing up in a world that often tries to diminish your potential, hope isn't just a wish; it's a choice. Through surrendering to God's plan and following Jesus' example, hope becomes the fuel that drives you forward, even when life feels stacked against you. Jesus' resurrection shows us that even when things look dead, hope can rise again when we trust a higher power.

To every Black boy and girl, know this: God made you with purpose, and nothing society says can take that from you. Surrender doesn't mean giving up—it means releasing the need to control everything and trusting that God has something greater in store. The world might try to limit you, but God's promise is limitless. When you surrender your doubts, fears, and setbacks, you open the door for God to work through you. With Jesus as your guide, your challenges become the soil where hope grows.

As you reach the end of this book, understand that true hope requires surrender—letting go of the things weighing you down and trusting that God's got you. Society often pushes self-reliance and control, but Jesus shows us that surrendering to a higher purpose unlocks real power. Through surrender, we realize that hope is not just about getting by—it's about transformation. The world is waiting for the unique gifts that God has placed inside of you, and by surrendering, you let those gifts flourish.

This is the message of The Autopsy of Hope: surrendering to God doesn't mean losing—it means letting hope lead the way. Jesus surrendered everything and, in doing so, showed us that even in the face of death, hope wins. Society may try to pull you down, but through surrender to God's purpose, you can rise above it. Today is the day to let go, let hope be reborn, and step fully into the purpose God has for you. The world needs you, Black boy, Black girl—don't keep us waiting. Surrender and let God's hope guide you to birth the change only you can bring. I believe in You. You're Necessary. You Matter!

Made in the USA
Columbia, SC
16 November 2024

0781d188-a2b2-4e26-91ff-3f6706f39d98R01